D0535792

American
WOMEN
in the Vietnam War

DIANE CANWELL and JON SUTHERLAND

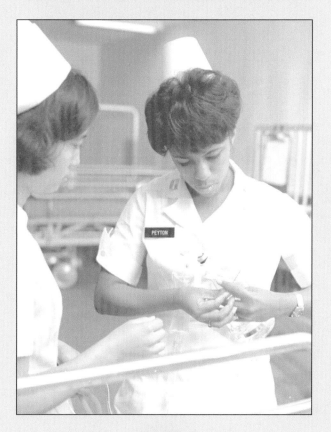

WORLD ALMANAC® LIBRARY

Please visit our web site at: www.worldalmanaclibrary.com
For a free color catalog describing World Almanac® Library's list of high-quality books
and multimedia programs, call 1-800-848-2928 (USA) or 1-800-387-3178 (Canada).
World Almanac® Library's fax: (414) 332-3567.

Library of Congress Cataloging-in-Publication Data

Sutherland, Jonathan.
    American women in the Vietnam War / by Jon Sutherland and Diane Canwell.
      p. cm. — (The American experience in Vietnam)
    Includes bibliographical references and index.
    ISBN 0-8368-5777-1 (lib. bdg.)
    ISBN 0-8368-5784-4 (softcover)
    1. Vietnamese Conflict, 1961-1975—Women—United States—Juvenile literature.
  I. Canwell, Diane. II. Title. III. Series.
  DS559.8.W6S87   2005
  959.704'3'0820973—dc22   2004058657

First published in 2005 by
World Almanac® Library
330 West Olive Street, Suite 100
Milwaukee, WI 53212 USA

Copyright © 2005 by World Almanac® Library.

Developed by Amber Books Ltd.
Editor: James Bennett
Designer: Colin Hawes
Photo research: Natasha Jones
World Almanac® Library editors: Mark Sachner and Alan Wachtel
World Almanac® Library art direction: Tammy West
World Almanac® Library production: Jessica Morris

Picture Acknowledgements
Cody Images (www.codyimages.com): cover (top left), 30; Corbis: 9, 17, 26, 28, 31, 32, 35, 38,
40, 42, 43; Getty Images: cover (main); U.S. National Archives: 1, 4, 8, 10, 20, 21, 22, 29, 36, 37;
The Women's Memorial Foundation: 6, 11, 12, 13, 15, 18, 24, 25.

Printed in Canada

1 2 3 4 5 6 7 8 9 09 08 07 06 05

About the Authors

JON SUTHERLAND and **DIANE CANWELL** have worked as a writing
team since 1990, writing for books and magazines on a wide range of historical
and military subjects. Jon Sutherland's publications include the 900-page
African Americans at War: An Encyclopedia, while Diane Canwell has authored
books on various aspects of military history. They live in Norfolk, U.K.

Table of Contents

Words that appear in the glossary are printed in **boldface** type
the first time they occur in the text

Introduction

The Vietnam War (1954–1975) was part of a larger conflict known as the Second Indochina War, which raged in Southeast Asia and involved the nations of Cambodia, Laos, and Vietnam. From 1946 until 1954, the Vietnamese had fought for independence from France during the First Indochina War. When the French were defeated, the country was divided into North and South Vietnam. Vietnamese **communists** controlled North Vietnam and wanted to unify Vietnam under communist rule. Non-communist Vietnamese controlled the South. In the 1950s, the United States and the Soviet Union were in the early years of their struggle over political, economic, and military influence in various parts of the world. Known as the Cold War, this struggle did not pit each nation against the other directly. Rather, each supported other countries that were squared off against one another. In the mid-1950s, the U.S. began training South Vietnam's army, while the Soviet Union and China backed communist North Vietnam. By the mid-1960s, U.S. forces fought alongside the Army of the Republic of Vietnam (ARVN) against the North Vietnamese Army (NVA) and the National Front for the Liberation of Vietnam (NLF).

The Vietnam War was not just a male experience. Although sources vary, it is estimated that between 7,500 and 11,000 women served in various branches of the military in Vietnam, the majority as nurses. An estimated 20,000 more worked for civilian aid organizations such as the American Red Cross, as entertainers with the United Service Organizations (USO), or as reporters and journalists. Some women traveled to Vietnam as librarians or worked for government organizations such as the Central Intelligence Agency (CIA) or the Department of

Defense. These women suffered some of the same hardships as the men in Vietnam, but they also had to cope with the challenges and frustrations of being a woman in a traditionally male-dominated field. Nurses, perhaps more so than any other group of women in Vietnam, were particularly vulnerable to dangers and attacks.

Naturally, women interacted with men in Vietnam. There were thousands more men serving than women, and for some this posed challenges. Some women had to deal with ridicule and scorn for wanting to participate in what was "a man's world;" others had to deal with harassment. Close bonds were forged, which sometimes led to relationships and even marriages. Other women had to cope with the fact that they had left their families at home while they served. Upon returning home, the women who had spent time in Vietnam found that sometimes returning to "normal life" was a difficult challenge. The American people had become strongly divided by the Vietnam War, and those who felt the United States had had no business being there often clashed with those who had supported the efforts of the troops. The Vietnam Women's Memorial was dedicated in 1993 as part of the Vietnam Veterans Memorial to honor the women who served in the United States armed forces and also to honor the families who lost loved ones in the war.

Below: This map shows North and South Vietnam and the surrounding area. Key regions, cities, and military bases are indicated.

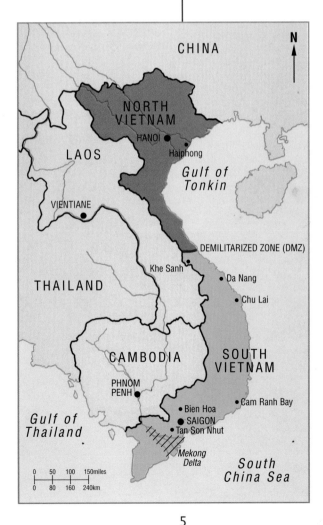

5

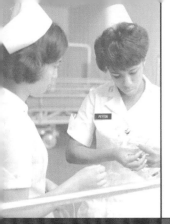

A Tough Job

Right: U.S. Army nurses at work at the Ninety-third Evacuation Hospital at Long Binh in 1968. The hospital operated between 1965 and 1971 and dealt with casualties from the central region of South Vietnam.

Women served in Vietnam in a wide variety of roles: in support staff assignments, in hospitals, on medical evacuation (MEDEVAC) flights, with mobile hospital units, operations groups, information offices, and headquarters offices, and in numerous other clerical, medical, intelligence, and personnel positions. These women—both officers and enlisted personnel—ranged from young women in their early twenties with barely two years of service to career military officers over the age of forty. Not only did these women often suffer the same hardships as men, but many of them also had to deal with the added pressures of being a woman in fields that were traditionally dominated by men. For example, a female journalist was asked by a U.S. Marine, "What did they send a woman here for? War is a man's business."

Accurate figures citing the number of women who served in Vietnam are difficult to find. According to the American War Library, during the United States' ten-year involvement in Southeast Asia, 5,905 military women served in Vietnam: 4,675 from the U.S. Army, 423 from the U.S. Navy, 36 from the Marine Corps, and 771 from the

USAID AND VIETNAM

During the Vietnam War, the United States set out not only to win military victory, but also to "win the hearts and minds" of the Vietnamese. To this end, a campaign was launched to bolster popular support for the South Vietnamese government against the communist North Vietnamese, providing assistance and development programs worth billions of dollars. The programs were directed by a government agency created to aid developing countries: the U.S. Agency for International Development, or USAID.

Between 1961 and 1972, USAID established hundreds of schools and health clinics in Vietnam, many of which were staffed by American women. USAID also provided hospitals, highways, and hydroelectric facilities to help the war-torn country.

The agency also sent thousands of agricultural experts, doctors, nurses, teachers, engineers, intelligence agents, and civilian advisers. For example, more than seven hundred U.S. physicians served tours in USAID-built South Vietnamese hospitals.

Above: The Women's Air Force (WAF) was a parallel service to the U.S. Air Force. Here, the first enlisted women are pictured at Tan Son Nhut airbase in June 1967. They were assigned to the Military Assistance Command, Vietnam, (MACV) in Saigon.

U.S. Air Force. In addition, there were the female members of the civil services and the Department of Defense. Other civilian aid organizations whose female members served in Vietnam include the American Red Cross, the Salvation Army, and the Young Women's Christian Association (YWCA).

LIFE IN VIETNAM

Women assigned to headquarters at Tan Son Nhut Air Force Base tended to work at least six and a half days a week, for ten to fifteen hours a day, with little time for recreation. Some had to wear their green cord uniforms on duty. Others wore lightweight **fatigues**, only wearing civilian clothes during their off-duty hours.

Most of the women cooked on hotplates in their rooms. There were no laundry facilities, but for $15 a month, a maid would clean the room and wash and press their uniforms. Lieutenant Colonel Elaine E. Filkins (USMC) recalled that her stockings did not last long, as the maids pounded them with rocks in the creek. Girdles, bras, and other lingerie did not survive this punishment for long either. When the weather was unusually wet or when the city was under attack, the women wore lightweight fatigues and **oxfords**. Enlisted women were exempt from income tax during their tour in Vietnam and officers received a $500 exemption. Like all military personnel, they had to convert their U.S. dollars into Military Payment Certificates—the only viable exchange in Vietnam.

In Saigon, the curfew was in force by 2000 or 2200 hours (8:00 or 10:00 P.M.) Popular leisure activities included bowling;

KEEPING THE GIs ENTERTAINED

Nancy Smoyer, a former Red Cross worker known as a "Donut Dollie," recalled playing games with troops: "It was our mission, our job, what we were sent to Vietnam to do. We played games in mess halls, on flight lines, in recreation centers, on LZ's (landing zones), firebases, along the road—wherever there were GIs. The games were usually a cross between a TV quiz show and a board game. We made them up with themes like sports, cars, the States, travel.... We'd gather the guys together, divide them into teams, and then pit them against each other, asking the teams questions as they tried to advance from point A to Z. For one game, we used children's alphabet blocks with which the men spelled out the answer by standing in line holding a block. My favorite part was at the end when I would say, 'Do you guys realize that you've just spent the last hour playing with kiddies' blocks?' The moans could be heard for miles."

Above: A former Red Cross worker attends the dedication of the Vietnam Women's Memorial Sculpture in Washington, D.C., on November 11, 1993.

watching old U.S. TV shows, which were broadcast for a few hours each night; or watching a movie at one of the camps or **billets**. Many women chose to use their spare time to help at orphanages or work for the Armed Forces Television Station. Some also taught English in Vietnamese schools.

THE WOMEN'S ARMY CORPS

The Women's Army Corps (WAC) was established on May 15, 1942, in response to a bill introduced in May 1941 by Massachusetts Congresswoman Edith Nourse Rogers for a women's **corps** in the Army. She originally envisioned a quasi-military organization of twenty-five thousand women to fill administrative and clerical jobs that the army would otherwise have given to enlisted men. Employing women in such jobs would make more men in the armed forces available for combat duties. With a further bill, she hoped to secure for women a salary and benefits package comparable to those of male soldiers. The organization was originally called the Women's Auxiliary Army Corps (WAAC); the Army dropped the "auxiliary" designation in 1943.

Between 1962 and 1973, seven hundred officers and enlisted women of the WAC served in Vietnam. Initially, most of the women were assigned to headquarters in Saigon (today known as

Right: WAC trainees march in formation at Fort McClellan in 1968. By June 1970, around 165 WAC officers and 1,500 enlisted women were on duty in the Far East.

WAC

Ho Chi Minh City) and were billeted at the Embassy Hotel. Saigon, the capital of South Vietnam, was always subject to attack from the Viet Cong, and this strategic location was a potentially hazardous place to work and live.

WACs assigned to the military hospital at Long Binh were housed in their own special compound within the base. The high fences around the compound were topped with barbed wire, not to keep out the Viet Cong but to protect the women from the advances of the men on the base.

Depending on their rank, there were from one to four women in each room in the barracks, which contained a simple army bed, a footlocker, and a dresser. Thick mosquito nets kept out insects, but they kept out fresh air, too. Outside were large corrugated iron bunkers, to be used in case of attacks on the base. Meals were eaten in communal mess halls within sight of the Twenty-fourth Evacuation Hospital and helicopters bringing in the wounded.

Above: Colonel, later Brigadier General, Elizabeth Hoisington (center left) visits a WAC detachment in Vietnam in 1967.

11

Many of the WACs were decorated for their service in Vietnam, receiving the Legion of Honor, Bronze Star Medal, and the Meritorious Service Medal to name a few. Captain Catherine A. Brajkovich received an Army Commendation Medal for heroism for alerting officers in Saigon of a fire in their building. Major Gloria A. S. Olson, a journalist and photographer, received the Air Medal for having flown in the equivalent of 127 aerial combat missions totalling 198 air hours during her tour in Vietnam. In 1978, shortly after the end of the Vietnam War, the WAC was disbanded, and from then on women were assigned to different branches of the army.

WOMEN IN THE U.S. MARINES

Only thirty-six female marines served in Vietnam during the war. Arrangements for their accommodation were not well organized at first. After enduring an eighteen-hour flight to Bien Hoa, north of Saigon, female Marines were billeted at the Ambassador Hotel and later moved to the Plaza Hotel. In 1968, they were transferred to the Billings Bachelor Enlisted Quarters, close to the Tan Son Nhut Airbase.

The first U.S. Marine Corps woman to serve in a combat theater, Master Sergeant Barbara J. Dulinsky, arrived at Bien Hoa Air Force Base on March 18, 1967. Most of the female marines served with the Marine Liaison/Marine Corps Personnel Section on the staff of the Commander, Naval Forces, Vietnam, but several others worked for the Military Assistance

Below: In March 1967, Master Sergeant Barbara Dulinsky, who had requested reassignment to Vietnam, was transferred to the MACV in Saigon. She was the first female marine to serve in a combat area.

Command, Vietnam (MACV), the Secretary of the General Staff (SGS), and the Adjutant General's Office.

WOMEN IN THE U.S. AIR FORCE

In 1966, the first sixteen female air force nurses arrived at Cam Ranh Bay, and by June 1967, the successful deployment of these personnel had brought a Women's Air Force (WAF) lieutenant colonel and five enlisted women to work at the MACV headquarters in Saigon. Others soon followed to work at the MACV and at the Seventh Air Force headquarters at Tan Son Nhut. More were deployed at Cam Ranh Bay and Bien Hoa. These women worked in logistics, public affairs, personnel, aircraft maintenance, photo interpretation, intelligence, administration, and meteorology. Air force women stationed in Vietnam numbered twenty officers and twenty-two enlisted women at their peak strength in June 1971. In all, between five hundrred and six hundred air force women served in Southeast Asia.

WAFs were given weapons courses and training, specifically on using the M-16 rifle. WAF nurses on air-evacuation duties in

12TH USAF
HOSPITAL
CAM RANH BAY AIR BASE

Left: The first women arrived in 1966 at the Twelfth U.S. Air Force hospital at Cam Ranh Bay. Later, nurses were assigned to Tan Son Nhut, Danang, and medical units in Thailand.

LIBRARIANS IN VIETNAM: ARMY SPECIAL SERVICES

The Army Special Services Program in Vietnam began on July 1, 1966. The program was operated by civilians, who volunteered to serve one-year tours. According to author Ann Kelsey, a civilian who worked for the U.S. Army in Vietnam (USARV) Special Services Library Branch from 1969 to 1970, the women who served as Special Services librarians and recreation specialists managed permanent libraries on some of the larger bases and supervised 250 field library units. They also arranged the distribution of 190,000 magazine subscriptions and 350,000 paperbacks. Because there were far fewer personnel than there were installations requiring their services, these Special Services librarians traveled by any available means: in Jeeps, trucks, helicopters, and fixed-wing aircraft, and on foot. They endured rocket attacks, mortar barrages, and commando raids against the installations at which they were located, sometimes spending nights in sandbagged, rat-infested bunkers.

Vietnam were often issued a **sidearm** for personal protection. According to authors Jeanne M. Holm, Major General (USAF, Ret.), and Sarah P. Wells, Brigadier General (USAF Nurse Corps, Ret.), the need for women to be able to handle weapons took on new meaning with the Tet Offensive. In the initial years of the Vietnam War, a tradition had been established of declaring a **truce** for a few days during Tet, the Vietnamese New Year, to allow people on both sides to celebrate. In January 1968, however, the communists announced a truce for the Tet holiday but then launched an attack on almost every major city and province in South Vietnam. Air force women earned praise from a senior master sergeant for their actions:

"What impressed me the most, with respect to the conduct of our personnel during the Tet Offensive, was the calm [with which] female service members went about their duties. That belief that the frail (or fair) sex will tremble at the first sign of trouble is not true."

Despite the encouraging words, however, some air force officials insisted that all WAF personnel be evacuated. In response, a WAF staff sergeant wrote to the Pentagon: "Don't let them send us home. I came here to do a job and I want to see it through." The air force request was turned down, and the WAF stayed in Vietnam.

WOMEN IN THE U.S. NAVY

The navy insisted that Vietnam was not a suitable assignment for women. A female officer could only be sent if a commanding officer asked for her by name and stated that she was qualified for the job. Things changed for female naval personnel in August 1972 when a trial program allowed a limited number of officers and enlisted women to be assigned to the crew of the hospital ship *Sanctuary*. Nonetheless, by the end of the Vietnam War, just nine female naval officers had served in Vietnam. Most were assigned to the naval staff in Saigon, and one reported to the Naval Support Activity in Cam Ranh Bay. No enlisted navy women served in Vietnam.

Below: Lieutenant Commander Elizabeth Barrett was the highest-ranking woman to serve in Vietnam. She commanded 450 enlisted men in the Naval Advisory Group.

The first female naval officer to report for duty in Vietnam was Lieutenant Elizabeth G. Wyle. She began work at the Command Information Center in Saigon in June 1967. Her duties included preparing reports and briefings for journalists and politicians. Wyle was unsure what to expect from the male officers, but she soon discovered that "The only difficulties encountered were the same as the men. We were all away from home, families, and not in a particularly pleasant situation."

Lieutenant Commander Elizabeth Barrett was the highest-ranking female navy officer to serve in Vietnam and the first woman in the navy to hold a command in a combat zone. She served

Right: Female members of the Vietnam Veterans of America (VVA), attend the dedication of the Vietnam Women's Memorial Sculpture in Washington, D.C., on November 11, 1993.

in Vietnam for fifteen months and had just three days off: "February 2, 1972, when I went sailing at Cet Lo; March 29, when I went swimming at Vung Tau; and December 19, when I wrote Christmas cards."

Although their number was small, the nine navy women who served in Vietnam had a significance far beyond their tiny number. Like hundreds of women in the other services, they made it impossible to deny that women other than nurses could serve in areas where they would be at risk from enemy action. Their competence, industry, and patriotism demonstrated that navy women were both ready and able to serve wherever they might be needed.

CIVILIAN AID ORGANIZATIONS

Many other women worked in Vietnam, although in civilian capacities, as nurses, singers, performers, recreational staff, librarians, and journalists. Four primary civilian aid organizations had members who volunteered in Vietnam: the American Red Cross, the Salvation Army, the YMCA, and the YWCA. Three categories of Red Cross personnel worked in Vietnam: SMH (Service to Military Hospitals), who worked in the hospitals with patients, doing a combination of social work and recreation therapy; SMI (Service to Military Installations), who arranged emergency leave and handled communications from the families back home regarding births, deaths, and emergencies; and SRAO (Supplemental Recreational Activities Overseas), also known as the Donut Dollies. These women provided "a touch of home in a combat zone." They brought games and Kool-Aid to the soldiers and helped them, even if only temporarily, to forget the horrors of war.

Like many Vietnam veterans, the women who served in Vietnam, whether military personnel or civilians, have found it difficult to forget their experiences there. Unlike their male counterparts, however, they have rarely been officially recognized. Some have kept their service a secret; many have been affected by post-traumatic stress disorders; others have suffered from chemical poisoning. Linda Watson, a WAC private, summed up the feelings of many: "I didn't think I qualified for benefits, because I didn't consider myself a Vietnam vet. It's just recently I came to the realization I am. I didn't see all the atrocities. But I saw enough for me."

POST-TRAUMATIC STRESS DISORDER AND VIETNAM

Ten years after her last trip to Vietnam, broadcaster Chris Noel began suffering from migraines, nightmares, and numbness in her arms and legs. She was initially treated for allergies and anxiety and became addicted to Valium. After attempting suicide, she spent three months in a psychiatric hospital. She recalled the harrowing events she had witnessed in Vietnam, but none of the doctors made the link between these experiences and her state of mind, and neither did they consider the suicide of her Green Beret husband shortly after returning from Vietnam.

Noel found out about an outreach program that aimed to help veterans readjust. She discovered that she was not alone in her feelings of depression, anxiety, and guilt about surviving the war. She finally discovered that she was a victim of post-traumatic stress disorder (PTSD), a condition first diagnosed in those who served in Vietnam and now estimated to have affected between 0.5 and 1.5 million veterans.

Female Nurses

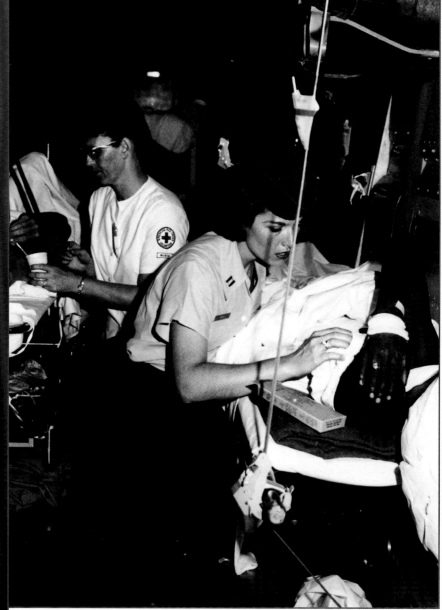

Right: A U.S. Air
Force flight nurse
and a Red Cross
nurse attend to the
wounded on board
a U.S. Air Force
C-141 in 1967. Air
medical evacuation
took place from
Tan Son Nhut
airbase directly to
specialized military
medical centers in
the U.S.

The nurses who served in Vietnam, both military and civilian, were among the unsung heroes of the war. They were vulnerable almost everywhere: in the hospitals, out in the field, and even in their barracks, or living quarters. Attacks were always a possibility. No matter what happened, however, the nurses handled it with grace and courage.

THE ARMY NURSE CORPS

The Army Nurse Corps (ANC) was founded in 1901 after Dr. Anita Newcomb McGee helped draft a bill to establish a nurse corps. The ANC is the oldest military nursing corps and was the first military organization to admit women. The ANC's mission, according to the U.S. Army's web site, "is to provide quality nursing service whether the need is for immediate deployment, sustained conflict, or any other healthcare mission."

The women of the ANC were among the first U.S. women to be sent to Vietnam. Three female nurses arrived in Saigon in April 1956. They were attached to the U.S. Army Medical Training Team (U.S. Military Assistance Advisory Group) to train South Vietnamese nurses. From 1962 to 1973, more than four thousand women from the ANC served in Vietnam. The majority of them were around twenty-three years old and were comparatively new to nursing. Indeed, just over one-third actually had any nursing experience. Most served the typical twelve-month tour, and most lived in tents, at least until 1967. Then, they were billeted in huts, or, if they were lucky, in air-conditioned trailers. As new hospitals were set up around South Vietnam, many of the newcomers found themselves housed in insect-infested, leaky, noisy, and humid old tents. In 1966, some of the nurses were assigned to medical, self-contained, transportable units, such as the Forty-fifth Surgical Hospital. These hospitals were rubber, transportable facilities with their own electricity, heating, air conditioning, and waste disposal.

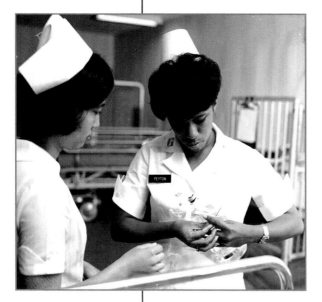

In practice, however, the mobile hospitals had to negotiate difficult terrain, were poorly maintained, and were always vulnerable to attack.

Although most of the nurses preferred to wear lightweight fatigues, some of the hospitals insisted that they wear white duty uniforms. Laundry facilities were basic, at best, and it was hard to keep the uniforms clean, so hospitals often gave in and allowed standard fatigues. Most of the ANC nurses worked a twelve-hour day, six days

Above: U.S. Army nurses work at the Third Field Hospital on July 12, 1971. Although staff at the Third Field Hospital wore the white duty uniform, most nursing personnel in Vietnam usually wore lightweight cotton olive drab fatigues.

PRAYER OF AN ARMY NURSE

Hear my prayer in silence before Thee as I ask for
  courage each day.
Grant that I may be worthy of the sacred pledge of
  my profession
And the lives of those entrusted to my care.
Help me to offer hope and cheer in the hearts of men
  and my country,
For their faith inspires me to give the world and nursing
  my best.
Instill in me the understanding and compassion of those
  who led the way,
For I am thankful to You for giving me this life to live.

Major (U.S. Army ret.) Mildred I. Clark, RN.

a week. Sleep was often considered to be the best recreation available. Many gave up their free time to help at orphanages or give childcare assistance to local villages.

Between January 1965 and December 1970, the ANC staff admitted some 133,447 wounded, of whom 97,659 needed hospitalization. Booby-traps, assault rifles, and rocket-propelled grenades caused terrible injuries, and frequently the wounds were infected by foul water from the rice paddy fields in Vietnam. Despite the hardships, however, the rewards were great, as one nurse, Shirley A. Purcell, recalled: "The teamwork and camaraderie extended out into the helicopter unit, the dust-off unit that was

Below: Medical staff remove field bandages at the Second Surgical Hospital, Lai Khe, in September 1969.

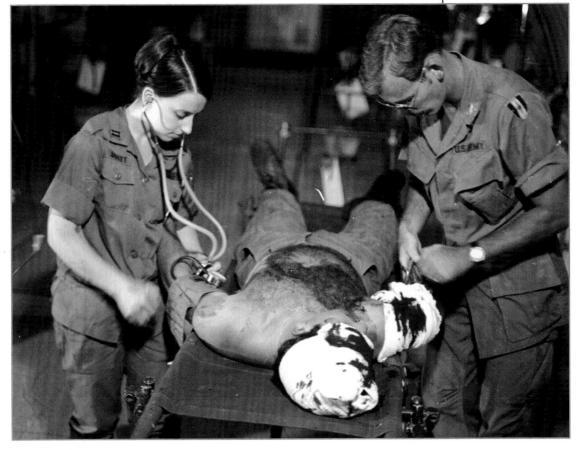

attached to the hospital, and into the other line units around us. We seemed to be the greatest contribution to morale because they knew they were going to be cared for if they were injured."

CIVILIAN NURSES IN VIETNAM

The female nurses who served in Vietnam were not just from the military. Plenty of civilian female nurses volunteered to spend time in Vietnam. They worked on behalf of such organizations as the Special Services, the Department of Defense, the Salvation Army, and the American Red Cross. Furthermore, these women did not all come from the United States. Around 210 Australian

Below: President Lyndon B. Johnson talks to nurses in Vietnam on December 23, 1967.

KEEPING A BALANCE

Anna Marie Rutallie, who served in the ANC at the Ninety-first Evac Hospital in Chu Lai from July 1970 to July 1971, recalled a humorous incident:

"To break the stress in the wards, we would pull practical jokes on each other and even on the patients. I remember this one guy, a six-footer from a Ranger company, who was in our hospital for malaria. This guy was a big chicken when it came to getting his blood drawn and needles in general. So one day, I thought I would play a joke on him, kind of a payback for all the time he gave me grief when I went to draw his blood. I took a 60-cc syringe, attached a six-inch spinal needle to it, and proceeded down to his bed. When he saw that contraption, his eyes just about bugged out, and he jumped off the bed and ran to the end of the ward. All the other guys in the ward laughed themselves silly. You know, I never had any more trouble out of that guy."

nurses traveled to South Vietnam between 1964 and 1972 to care for injured civilians during the war.

RED CROSS NURSES

Clara Barton helped establish the American Red Cross in Washington, D.C., on May 21, 1881, after she was impressed by the Swiss-inspired International Red Cross Movement. In 1900, Congress granted the American Red Cross a charter, whereby it was allowed to provide services to members of the U.S. armed forces and relief to disaster victims at home and abroad.

The first American Red Cross staff members were sent to

Vietnam in February 1962. From then until March 1973, official figures indicate that some 1,120 women served. Around 627 of the women belonged to the Red Cross's SRAO program. Others served in the SMH or SMI. Aside from running recreational programs for the troops, these women shared many of the dangers other U.S. personnel faced in Vietnam. Five female Red Cross workers died during the war between 1961 and 1971, and many more were injured.

THE TOUGHEST JOB IN VIETNAM

The Vietnam Women's Memorial was established not only to honor the more than 265,000 women who served in the United States armed forces during the war, both in Vietnam and the U.S., but also for the families who lost loved ones in the war. People would know about the women who provided comfort and care for those who were suffering and dying. The Vietnam Women's Memorial was dedicated in 1993 as part of the Vietnam Veterans Memorial. During the campaign to have the Women's Memorial approved for erection at the Arlington National Cemetery in Washington, D.C., U.S. Navy Vietnam veteran Joe Muharsky wrote to the founder of the memorial project, Diane Carlson Evans: "I did my share of killing and I saw my share of dying, but I want you to know that before I ever heard of your cause I was giving a talk to high school students, and

Below: A U.S. Navy nurse serves in the intensive care unit of a hospital ship, USS *Repose*, in October 1967. The vessel was stationed south of the seventeenth parallel in the South China Sea, off the coast of South Vietnam.

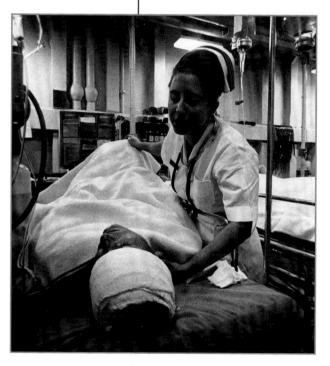

after I told them my story, as bad as it was, I asked them a question. I asked the students what they thought was the toughest job in Vietnam. Not one of them had the same answer I did. I told them I thought it was being a nurse."

Lieutenant Colonel Janis A. Nash summed up the experience of many nurses who served in Vietnam: "I'm no heroine. I joined the Army Nurse Corps to go to Europe, that's what my recruiter promised me. I was twenty-one years old when I was ordered to Vietnam. I stayed 364 days. I cared for the sick, the wounded, and the dying. I did the best I could. I am only coming to know that now."

ALL IN A DAY'S WORK

In addition to caring for battlefield casualties, nurses cared for soldiers and Vietnamese civilians who had fallen victim to tropical diseases, such as bubonic plague, dengue fever, typhoid, jungle rot, and cholera. Other accidents and injuries that brought soldiers to U.S. military hospitals included "friendly fire" mishaps, attempted suicides, drug overdoses, drownings, monkey bites, and attacks by tigers. Nurses were also expected to serve as assistants during evacuation procedures in the event of rocket or mortar attacks.

Left: U.S. Army nurse Captain Elizabeth Finn helps out at an orphanage in 1967. In their spare time, nurses also ran free medical services for the civilian population, helping to "win the hearts and minds" of the Vietnamese people.

Entertainers

Right: Bob Hope and Raquel Welch entertain the troops in December 1967. Hollywood entertainers played a vital role in helping to maintain and bolster the morale of troops during the conflict.

Given the violence and death that the soldiers had to deal with in Vietnam, not to mention the fact that they were far from home, those who worked in Vietnam in the performing arts were crucial to upholding the morale of the nurses, pilots, soldiers, and others they entertained.

THE USO

The USO (United Service Organizations) was formed in 1941 at the request of President Franklin D. Roosevelt. It brought together six civilian agencies: the Salvation Army, the YMCA, the YWCA, the National Catholic Community Services, the National Travelers Aid Association, and the National Jewish Welfare Board. The first USO club in Vietnam opened in Saigon in 1963. During the war, an additional seventeen centers were opened elsewhere in Vietnam, and a further six were opened in Thailand. The USO clubs offered snack bars, barbershops, gift shops, an overseas telephone line, photo labs, and the much-sought-after hot showers. The familiar, red, white, and blue USO sign, with its six stars to signify the six agencies involved, brought Christmas parties, barbecues, fast food, newspapers, and a friendly atmosphere to the troops so far from home. During the war, about 5,559 performances were organized. Legendary comedian Bob Hope had been entertaining troops at home and abroad for years when the Vietnam War

BOBBIE THE WEATHER GIRL

Introduced on TV as "the bubbling bundle of barometric brilliance," Bobbie the Weather Girl was a welcome ray of sunshine to the soldiers. On her weather show, she entertained the audience with jokes and skits and danced to songs like "Proud Mary." Bobbie spent an extensive amount of time visiting soldiers out in the field, boosting their morale. On her show, Bobbie often extended greetings to men who had written in or to the units she had visited. Bobbie closed each show with a wink and wished "everyone a pleasant evening weather-wise and good wishes for other-wise."

began, so it was only natural that he take his USO Christmas Show to Vietnam in 1964. In 1997, Congress designated Bob Hope an honorary veteran for his humanitarian services to the United States armed forces, making him the only individual in history to have earned this honor.

Many young women signed up for eighteen-month tours with the USO as singers or dancers. The women were not required to wear uniforms, aside from the outfits they wore when performing. Each of the volunteers was given the rank of honorary captain by the Department of Defense. Actress and singer Connie Stevens was one of the many women who toured Vietnam: "Forty-two thousand vets were in the audience in Vietnam. When I was introduced, the sound from the crowd was almost deafening. When I started 'Silent Night' everyone started singing and crying, swaying back and forth."

Priscilla Mosby toured as a USO bandleader between 1970 and 1972. She recalls the excitement of putting on shows in Vietnam: "We performed for three hours. I was the only female out there

Right: Connie Stevens sings at one of the annual Bob Hope Vietnam Christmas Shows on December 28, 1969. The cast performed in front of some twenty thousand U.S. troops at Long Binh amphitheatre, 10 miles (16 kilometers) north of Saigon.

COLONEL MAGGIE

Left: Martha Raye performs in Danang on October 16, 1965. Raye became known as "Colonel Maggie" and toured Vietnam extensively, often at her own expense, for several years.

In May 1965, actress Martha Raye, dubbed "Colonel Maggie" by the troops, began the first of her eight tours in Vietnam. She had received basic nursing training in the 1930s and had brushed up her skills in Korea. In 1967, she found her nursing skills in great need when the camp medic was hit during a large-scale attack on the Special Forces camp at Soc Trang. For several hours, the camp was in great danger of being overrun. The military tried to send in helicopters to evacuate Raye and the wounded, but poor weather and heavy fighting prevented any such missions. Raye worked tirelessly throughout the action, dealing with the wounded in the operating theater for around thirteen hours.

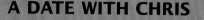

A DATE WITH CHRIS

Above: Chris Noel broadcasts on U.S. Forces Radio in 1966. Noel also traveled to even the most remote areas to boost the morale of the troops.

Chris "Miss Christmas" Noel broadcast her "Date with Chris" program on Armed Forces Radio to military personnel around the world and was extremely popular in Vietnam, where she made regular visits. December 25 was always Noel's busiest day. Dressed in a mini-skirted version of a Santa outfit, she visited as many firebases and landing zones as possible. She recalled how the show got started:

"I wanted to go. Desperately, I wanted to go with Bob Hope. The minute I got this radio show, I volunteered to go, and I was told I couldn't. I was turned down. I just wasn't a big enough star. But then, weeks later, I received a telegram. It said 'Chris Noel, we would like you to go to Vietnam to help build up the morale of the troops.' "

Noel toured Vietnam by helicopter, singing and dancing to thousands of troops between 1966 and 1970. On many occasions her life was at risk:

"I remember one time when we were on top of a mountain and there was incoming and I was flat up against the bunker as they brought in a helicopter to get me out. I was really scared. As it landed, I didn't get in that helicopter; I was literally thrown into it, and I heard the bullets hitting it as we took off."

in the field. We had some wild times. The main thing I kept in mind was to be decent and dedicated and determined to let them know that it was going to be all right. They could let off steam, singing and dancing and pouring beer on me." When Mosby and her band were in Binh Thuy in the Mekong Delta, however, tragedy struck while she was out shopping alone in a local town. Mosby was caught in an air attack and had to take shelter in a nearby restaurant. "I got back to the base and someone told me that the bunker had been hit. My guys—the barracks they were in—were totally demolished. My entire band had been killed."

The role of the USO brought a welcome sense of home to the troops stationed in Vietnam. Although the likes of Bob Hope, Bing Crosby, and other stars linger uppermost in the veterans' minds, the thousands of unknown entertainers kept the enormous undertaking going through the hardest times in Vietnam.

Left: Actress and singer Ann-Margret appears with General Creighton Williams Abrams, the vice chief of staff of the U.S. Army, on stage at the Bob Hope Christmas Show at Long Binh in 1966. Abrams later succeeded General William Westmoreland as commander in chief in Vietnam in 1967.

Relationships

Right: Lieutenant Kathleen Rockwell sits with her husband, Lieutenant Richard Rockwell, at Qui Nhon on September 13, 1965. Kathleen managed to get a transfer to a field hospital near her husband, but he was soon sent back into action at Cam Ranh Bay.

Outnumbered by the thousands of male service personnel, women in Vietnam had to play a number of often contradictory roles, from mother, sister, and confidante to sweetheart. Serious relationships between soldiers and American women in Vietnam were not common, however. The men from the front lines simply craved the company of an American woman to remind them of home.

WOMEN AND MEN

The huge disparity in numbers between women and men in Vietnam could have created a combustible cocktail of pent-up feelings. However, according to WAC First Sergeant Marion C. Crawford, "the intelligent ones [men] treated us well." For the most part, male soldiers felt compelled to protect the WACs, and during attacks on Long Binh, where Crawford was stationed, the troops would surround the women's barracks. There were examples of the men trying to make life easier for the women. Crawford recalled: "They [the male soldiers] bent over backwards to bring us treats, anything to make us feel comfortable. One first sergeant stole a bathtub out of a French house.... I told him women like baths; they don't like showers. Not two days later, a tank comes right up with a big old French bathtub on top."

The attention, however, could be more than the women could take or took on forms that the women found unacceptable, as Karen Offnut, who also served at Long Binh, recounted: "I worked for several generals—they just treated me like a daughter. One was especially concerned.... He would never get any hint of impropriety. The rest were pretty nice. I was a hard worker. I remember....this one colonel put his arm around me and kept putting his arms around me, and I spun around and said 'I'll knock you flat if you do that again.'" Linda J. McClenahan, a nurse who served at Long Binh, described the attentions of the

AMERASIAN CHILDREN

As the war escalated, the number of male troops in Vietnam rocketed. As the numbers of troops increased, so did the number of relationships between Vietnamese women and soldiers. As a result, there was a large population of Amerasian children in Vietnam. Across the whole of South Vietnam, there was not a single village without Amerasian children. Their fathers ranged from generals to privates, from civilian construction workers to aides at the U.S. embassy. Estimates suggest that at least 50,000 children were born from relationships between U.S. citizens and Vietnamese women. Unfortunately, many thousands of these children were left behind when their fathers returned to the United States. In December 1987, Congress passed the Amerasian Homecoming Act. It allowed 23,643 people presumed to have been born from one of these relationships between January 1962 and January 1976, along with their 63,912 dependents, to go to the United States. The initial acceptance rate was around 90 percent. By the mid-1990s, the acceptance rates had dropped, and in 2002, only 23 were granted **visas** from a high of 19,000 in 1989.

uniformed men as being a "fine line between flattering popularity and sexual harassment."

MILITARY MOMS

A few WACs were forced to leave Vietnam as a result of pregnancy. Some fourteen married women were sent to Vietnam between 1967 and 1973. Eight of these women were pregnant on

Left: An Amerasian holds his child at a Ho Chi Minh City transit camp, awaiting passage to the U.S. in 1995. The word "Amerasian" dates back to the early 1950s and has been used primarily with reference to children fathered in Asia by U.S. servicemen.

OPERATION BABY LIFT

One of the most harrowing episodes of the war took place in April 1975 as South Vietnam crumbled under the attacks from the North Vietnamese. On April 3, 1975, President Gerald Ford announced Operation Baby Lift, which was aimed at evacuating an estimated 70,000 orphans. In the end, only around 2,000 children were flown to the United States and 1,200 to other locations, including Canada and Europe. Some of the remaining orphans were to become part of the mass exodus of 132,000 refugees that fled Vietnam in 1975.

their arrival and were sent straight back to the U.S. In the period between January 1967 and September 1968, 225 single WACs were sent to Vietnam, and five became pregnant and were sent home for discharge. Army regulations stated that a woman would be involuntarily discharged as soon as she became pregnant, and if an unmarried woman had an abortion prior to her discharge date, she, too, would be discharged. In April 1970, the rules were changed, however, and abortions could be performed if the life or health of the mother was in danger.

RELATIONSHIPS WITH THE VIETNAMESE

Soldiers naturally came in regular contact with Vietnamese women. The majority of such women were peasants, menial employees, or prostitutes. The very nature of the Vietnamese language limited communication to perhaps a dozen words of **pidgin**. There was also an enormous cultural gap. For security reasons, Vietnamese civilian areas were generally off-limits to U.S. troops. While some soldiers met and even married Vietnamese women, the military strongly discouraged such relationships.

ORPHANAGES

U.S. personnel had a long association with Vietnamese orphanages. Many female nurses and other military staff spent much of their free time working in and funding these establishments. Kathy Oatman served as an administration sergeant at Long Binh between February 1969 and May 1972 and recalled the attachment of U.S. units and

individuals to many of the children in orphanages: "Most groups over there sponsored an orphanage one way or another. [When] we went into the Tam Mai orphanage, I got attached to one little boy there [Kevin].... My commanding officer asked me 'What are you going to do about Kevin? If you don't get started, you won't be able to get that baby out of the country.'"

Oatman managed to adopt Kevin, and after a visit to the World Vision Hospital, she adopted a second child, Kimmy. For Oatman and her two children, like many hundreds of others, the adoption and the new life in the United States worked, as Oatman explained: "In the town we used to live in, there was a little Vietnamese lady who used to run the alterations shop. Kimmy went in there one day, and the lady asked her if she ever wanted to see her real mother. And she pointed out to the car to me, and said, 'That's my real mother. That's the only mother I know.'"

Above: U.S. Marine Staff Sergeant Ermelinda Salazar (later Esquibel) touched the lives of Vietnamese orphans and was nominated for the 1970 Unsung Heroine Award sponsored by the Veterans of Foreign Wars Auxiliary.

Reporting Back

Right: United Press International reporter Betsy Halstead learns to fire an M-14 rifle at Khe Sanh on August 20, 1965. Shortly after this photograph was taken, Halstead was forced to use the weapon in defense when the Viet Cong attacked the outpost.

Women were not only serving the war effort in Vietnam, they were also covering it as journalists and reporters. Upon arriving home, the women who had spent time in Vietnam, whether as a soldier, a civilian aid worker, or as a reporter, found that sometimes returning to "normal life" was a difficult challenge.

JOURNALISTS

The first female journalists arrived in Vietnam in 1961. Some were sent as accredited journalists by newspapers, magazines, and TV networks, but others made the trip under their own steam. Journalists were entitled to free military transportation, access to military commanders, food, shelter, combat clothing, boots, and the use of a **telex**.

Upwards of two hundred women journalists, photographers, **stringers**, and **freelancers**, both for and against the war, experienced women and those determined to make a name for themselves, climbed on board commercial flights to Saigon. It was relatively easy to get a visa; just a handful of letters from U.S. newspapers secured accreditation. In June 1967, Jurate Kazickas, working as a researcher for *Look* magazine, was told she had no hope of being sent to Vietnam. She had no money, but she managed to get on to the game show *Password* and won five hundred dollars. She bought a one-way ticket to Saigon and worked as a freelance journalist in the combat zone.

In June 1967, a chance encounter nearly ruined women's chances of reporting from the combat zone in Vietnam. Denby Fawcett was working for the *Honolulu Advertiser* and was in a remote U.S. Army base in the Central Highlands. She happened to be there when the commanding general of U.S. forces, William Westmoreland, arrived for an inspection by helicopter. The base had just been attacked, and there were more than sixty casualties.

Below: Tracy Wood, a United Press International correspondent, covers the release of U.S. prisoners of war in Hanoi on March 14, 1972.

Among the crowd, Westmoreland spotted Fawcett. She was the daughter of his wife's friend, and when Westmoreland discovered that Fawcett had been at the base for several days, he produced a directive, ordering that civilian women could not stay overnight in a combat zone. It was impossible for a female reporter to fly out to the combat zone, follow up a story, and fly back in a day. Luckily, the female reporters lobbied successfully for the directive to be rescinded.

Below: Tracy Wood, a United Press International correspondent, covers the release of U.S. prisoners of war in Hanoi on March 14, 1972.

In some respects, female journalists had distinct advantages. When a crowd of eager journalists clamored to get on board helicopters heading out to the combat zone, places were often limited, but the crews were always eager to take a woman. In the early years, women also had the advantage of appearing less threatening when covering stories, particularly when they interviewed Vietnamese women and children. Others, however, shied away from the human-interest aspect of the conflict which women were stereotypically expected to cover, preferring the combat zone. ABC-TV correspondent Anne Morrissy Merick was one journalist who quickly realized that her softer reports were often cut and not used.

OTHER WOMEN IN VIETNAM

Among the estimated twenty thousand civilian women who volunteered for service in Vietnam, some worked for the Special Service, the Red Cross, the USO, the State Department, USAID, and the Central Intelligence Agency (CIA). The exact numbers of civilian women in Vietnam who worked in various intelligence and surveillance roles for the Department of Defense and the CIA may never be precisely known.

One of the most remarkable women who went to Vietnam was Ann Caddell Crawford, who arrived in Saigon with her three young children in 1963. Her husband was serving in the U.S. Army,

A WAR REPORTER'S FEARS

Claire Starnes, at Long Binh and Saigon between 1969 and 1971, commented on the continual fear of being captured by the Viet Cong. She was a translator and photojournalist:

"The biggest fear was to be taken prisoner. Can you imagine what kind of nightmare in terms of public relations it would have been? What a coup for the NV [the North Vietnamese]? "Apparently in 1968, military intelligence had gotten a document off a North Vietnamese that they were offering a $25,000 reward for a white American female. Our own government gave us life insurance which was worth only $10,000. We laughed about it, because, boy, we were worth more to the NV."

41

ON THE FRONT LINE

Journalist Dickey Chapelle was the first U.S. female journalist to die in Vietnam. She had won her paratroopers badge learning to make combat drops with the 101st Airborne, and habitually wore a pink flower in her bush hat. She told a friend, "I suppose my luck will run out some day. But if you're scared, really scared, you don't belong over here." On November 4, 1965, Chapelle, on assignment for the *National Observer*, was killed while out on patrol with U.S. Marines near Chu Lai.

and Crawford taught English in a number of schools in the capital. She experienced Vietnam, its people, and traditions firsthand and later wrote *Customs and Culture of Vietnam*. It was issued to all U.S. military personnel entering Vietnam; the book can still be bought in Vietnam in bootleg form, faithfully reproduced down to the last detail.

FORGOTTEN SERVICE

Vietnam provided both the familiar and the unfamiliar. Within the vast U.S. compounds, the U.S.-influenced cities, and the army camps, there was a sense of the United States within a foreign land. For those venturing out into the country, however, the culture and the realities of war would stay with them forever. According to author Sara Evans, women were among the Vietnam War veterans who returned home to a country that wanted to forget the experience. Still excluded from combat duty, women served extensively in the armed forces and especially in military hospitals. Their service was rendered invisible by the presumption that soldiers (and war) are male-oriented. Not until the 1990s was their service recognized and memorialized.

"HANOI JANE"

Actress Jane Fonda caused a great deal of controversy—and anger—when she toured North Vietnam in 1972, posing for photographs with communist troops and broadcasting on Radio Hanoi. Years later, when released POWs described the torture and degradation they suffered at the hands of the North Vietnamese, Fonda called them "hypocrites and liars." Fonda's views earned her the nickname "Hanoi Jane" among the POWs and other Vietnam veterans. Fonda delivered a televised apology to Vietnam veterans and their families in 1988, admitting that her actions had been "thoughtless and careless."

Left: U.S. actress Jane Fonda visits the Truong Dinh Residential Center in Nia Ba Trung, Hanoi, on July 18, 1972.

Time Line

1955: October, South Vietnam officially becomes the Republic of Vietnam (RVN).

1956: First female nurses arrive in Vietnam from the United States to train South Vietnamese nurses.

1962: First American Red Cross staff members are sent to Vietnam.

1964: August, USS *Maddox* is reportedly attacked by North Vietnamese in Gulf of Tonkin; Congress passes the Gulf of Tonkin Resolution.

1965: May, actress Martha Raye ("Colonel Maggie") begins first of her eight tours of Vietnam; November, journalist Dickey Chappelle becomes the first female journalist to die in Vietnam.

1966: First female U.S. Air Force nurses arrive at Cam Ranh Bay; July, Army Special Services program begins.

1967: First female naval officer reports for duty in Vietnam.

1968: January, Tet Offensive is launched.

1970: Widespread demonstrations protest the war; December, Congress repeals the Gulf of Tonkin Resolution.

1972: U.S. Navy assigns first female officers and enlisted women to the hospital ship *Sanctuary*; Jane Fonda tours North Vietnam, earning her the nickname "Hanoi Jane."

1973: January, peace accords are signed in Paris, France; March, last U.S. ground troops leave Vietnam.

1975: January, North Vietnam announces an all-out offensive to seize South Vietnam; April, Operation Baby Lift is enacted; last U.S. citizens are evacuated from Saigon; North Vietnamese take Saigon the next day.

Glossary

billet: an assigned lodging for military personnel

communist: someone who believes in a totalitarian system of government in which a single authoritarian party controls state-owned means of production

corps: an organized subdivision of the military

fatigues: the uniform or work clothing worn in the field

freelancer: a person who pursues a profession without a long-term commitment to any one employer

oxfords: loose trousers made of soft durable cotton

pidgin: a simplified form of speech containing vocabulary from two or more languages, used for communication between people who do not share a common language

sidearm: a small weapon such as a revolver worn at the side or in the belt

stringer: a reporter who works for a publication or news agency on a part-time basis

telex: a communication service involving teletypewriters connected by wire through automatic exchanges

truce: suspension of fighting by agreement of opposing forces

visa: an endorsement made on a passport by the proper authorities denoting that it has been examined and that the bearer may proceed into a country

Further Reading

BOOKS

Gruzit-Hoyt, Olga. *A Time Remembered: American Women in the Vietnam War*. New York: Presidio Press/Ballantine Books, 1999.

Norman, Elizabeth. *Women at War: The Story of Fifty Military Nurses Who Served in Vietnam*. Philadelphia: University of Pennsylvania Press, 1990.

Steinman, Ron. *Women in Vietnam*. New York: TV Books, Inc., 2000.

Walker, Keith. *A Piece of My Heart: The Stories of 26 American Women Who Served in Vietnam*. New York: Presidio Press/Ballantine Books, 1997.

WEB SITES

All About Women in Vietnam

www.illyria.com/vnwomen.html

This site includes accounts by and information on women who served in Vietnam, both civilian and military.

Military Women in Vietnam

userpages.aug.com/captbarb/femvetsnam.html

Facts, figures, and additional links about the women who served.

In-Country Women

grunt.space.swri.edu/women.htm

This site is devoted to the military nurses and civilian women who died in Vietnam.

The Vietnam Women's Memorial

www.nps.gov/vive/memorial/women.htm

See photos and read the history of how this important monument came into being.

Index